A Catholic Bishop Teaches...

God's Plan for You:
Understanding Your Personal Vocation

Most Reverend
Fabian Bruskewitz

BASILICA ™

P R E S S

Published by
Basilica Press
111 Ferguson Court, Ste. 102
Irving, TX 75062

Editor: Mary Gottschalk
Cover design: Giuliana Gerber

Printed in the United States of America
ISBN 1-930314-20-5

Basilica Press is part of the
Joseph and Marie Daou Foundation.

TABLE OF CONTENTS

1. What does "vocation" mean?

A vocation is a call. The English word derives from the Latin verb *vocare*, which means "to call." A vocation is a call from God Himself.

2. What is a vocation?

Being a call, a vocation is a summons, an invitation; an indication from God about His will for us is what a vocation is. God, our heavenly Father, issues a call to us, sometimes by direct inspiration, but most often through the instrumentality by which He saves us, which is to say, through Jesus Christ, His divine Son, Who is His mercy, His wisdom, and His salvation made visible to us. This person who is Mercy, Wisdom, and Salvation is conferred through and in the third Person of the Blessed Trinity, God the Holy Spirit.

3. Does everyone have a vocation or do you have to be someone special?

A general vocation, summons, invitation is issued by God to every human being. In Christ and through the Holy Spirit, all are called to salvation, which is to say, all are called to the Catholic Church; all are called to the narrow way to heaven (see Mt 7:13–14 and *Catechism of the Catholic*

Church, I). God, however, Who created our human race in such a way as to endow mankind with the great gift of freedom, does not impose His will on the human race in a way that thwarts the use of that freedom. And although the human race is marred and seared and scalded by the horrors of original sin and actual sin, God's grace gives to all that which is necessary for appropriately answering His call. Thus, to every human being who accepts, at least in an implicit way, God's call and summons to faith and to the Catholic Church, the gift of salvation is offered. This gift is always given, but it is only bestowed when it is freely accepted, that is, when a person responds with God's grace to this call, this vocation. When people accept their calling, then God's chosen people of the New Testament are, both individually and together, summoned to holiness. Pope Benedict XVI cites in this regard I Peter 2:9, saying, "In Christ, the Head of the Church, which is his Body, all Christians form 'a chosen race, a royal priesthood, a holy nation, God's own people, that you may declare the wonderful deeds of him.'"

The Pope notes that the Catholic Church is holy even though it is composed of members who are always in need of purification. The Church is sinless, but composed, paradoxically, of sinful people. The holiness of the Catholic Church is a gift from God; He gave it to ensure that holiness in general may shine out to the human race with its full brightness. The Pope says, "The Second Vatican Council highlights the universal call to holiness, when it affirms: 'The followers of Christ are called by God, not because of their works, but according to his own purpose and grace. They are justified in the Lord Jesus, because in the Baptism of faith they truly become sons of God and sharers in the divine nature. In this way, they are really made holy' (*Lumen Gentium,* 40). Within the framework of this universal call, Christ, the High Priest, in his solicitude for the Church calls persons in every generation who are to care for his people. In particular, he calls to the ministerial priesthood men who are to exercise a fatherly role, the source of which is within the very fatherhood of God (see Eph 3:14)."

4. Why does God have a vocation for each of us?

Human beings are the crown of God's visible creation. By His design and plan, they are to share in His divine nature and end up happy forever with Him in heaven. It is in this plan of God, also called the divine economy of salvation, that God wishes each of us to be situated in a particular place, in a particular time, in a particular way. Just as a garden is more beautiful if it is composed of a great variety of flowers arranged in an orderly pattern, so the garden of God's visible creation is, by His intention, to be arranged in a way that encloses and includes a variety of vocations to shine forth to God His glory and His splendor and His goodness.

5. How do I know that God's plans are better than mine?

The ability to discern God's intentions for us is something that can fully be had only from the perspective of eternity; they will be thoroughly known to us only after we are united to God in heaven. His divine Providence, however, and His omniscience make it foolish for us even to begin to pretend that we would know better than God about anything, and certainly about our own lives and our own destinies. The image that Sacred Scripture uses of the potter and the clay that the potter uses to form various kinds of vessels is most appropriate for us to use when we think of God's plans and designs for us in the economy of salvation. The clay, as Saint Paul says, cannot speak back to the potter, or tell the potter how to form or shape the vessel (see Rom 9:19–24). As the Scriptures tell us and the hymn expresses, "He is the Potter, and we are the clay" (see Is 64:7).

6. How do I know that God's plans are better than the ones of the people who love me?

The people who express their love for us might sometimes not have a love that is truly authentic. Their love for us might be more a disguise for a type of selfishness or personal aggrandizement than a truly detached concern for our happiness in time and in eternity. No one can love us more than our heavenly Father does in Christ Jesus through the Holy Spirit. His intense love will burn away, if we let it, all human affections and loves that might stand in the way of what He plans for us—and it is in our best interests to let it. Those impeding satisfactions deriving from human love are not even slightly comparable to the satisfactions that come from our conforming to what God wants for us and intends for us. Love is not measured by sentiment, ardor, passion, or emotion. True love is measured only by sacrifice; and God, Who gives Himself to us in Christ, Who sacrificed Himself on the cross on our behalf, presents to us the most authentic form and type of love, surpassing all others. This is why Jesus said, "Greater love no one has than one who lays down his life for his friends," and "God so loved the world that He gave His only-begotten Son" (Jn 15:13 and 3:16).

7. Would following the rules of the Church be enough to be saved?

First, it must be remembered that being a Catholic

is more than just following rules and commandments. It means being joined to Christ. It means sharing in God's life and God's nature through sanctifying grace. Salvation, in the final and ultimate sense, is a freely given gift of God, not something we do, as much as something that God bestows on us all, undeserving as we may be. It is true that we must conform to God's will and conform our will to His, and that doing so does necessarily include obeying laws, rules, regulations, the commandments of God and the commandments of the Church. However, as the Council of Trent put it, God permits and allows His gifts to be called our merits (*Decree on Justification*, chapter 16).

That being said, we should keep in mind that certain vocations, and positive responses to them, are incumbent upon us. But there are, on the other hand, also some vocations that go beyond those things which are required. They are simply in the measure and the tone of an invitation, the rejection of which could result in our experiencing less happiness in this world and in eternity than we otherwise would be. In short, all are required to respond to the call of God to faith, to the Church, to Baptism, and to the call, the universal vocation from God, to holiness. Within that general call there are a number of other calls or summonses or vocations. These vocations to states in life, and to particular areas of work and activity, are, for the most part, simply invitations, and if one were not to discern properly or follow completely these invitations, these calls, these particular vocations from God, this would not imperil one's eternal salvation. Nevertheless, such a refusal, to put it in human terms, would be a disappointment in one's own life and externally a disappointment to God. Why, you ask? It would be a disappointment because one would be rejecting the precious treasure of that special kind of vocation God wanted to give to him or her.

8. What do I need to find my vocation?

The answer is that, first of all, one needs a relationship with God, a relationship rooted in prayer. One also needs a relationship of close intimacy that comes with the devout reception of our Lord in the Holy Eucharist, with a devout and conscientious participation in the dying and rising of Jesus, which we experience at every Mass, and from taking advantage of the abiding presence of Christ in our midst in the Blessed Sacrament reserved in the tabernacles of our Catholic churches. Prayer is the most likely place whereat one would find a vocation, and also the most likely venue for the clearest perception of that call.

There are, however, both internal and external indications of vocations. Sometimes the external indication of a vocation can come from the example and even the words of the people around us. Parents, friends, and others—teachers, priests, religious whom we encounter, as well as various kinds of close friends—can sometimes be the instruments of God's grace, pointing us in the direction that His plans call for us to go.

Then there is the importance of the internal movements that God the Holy Spirit will put into our hearts and into our minds as we go along in our lives. To be able to be attentive to these inclinations and inspirations of the Holy Spirit, we need to give ourselves time for quiet reflection on the whole idea of a vocation. This is why such tactics as going on a retreat or scheduling daily times of quiet meditation can be so valuable in the work of discernment.

9. When is the right moment to start discerning my vocation?

God calls us, within the context of the general and universal call to holiness, at various times in life. Sometimes He indicates to someone of a very tender age the direction that He wants that person to go; such an indication can be picked up and discerned by a delicate and prayerful spirit, and become their focus in life at an early time.

On the other hand, there are those who, because of their personalities and their psychological makeup, and because of God's will, will find their vocation only at later stages in their lives. People can be called to marriage, or to a dedicated single life in the world, or to the priesthood or the consecrated religious life, at all kinds of different times—in grade school, high school, college, even after a time of life lived in some occupation, profession, or activity that is not the ultimate direction of a person's life. It depends basically on God's good pleasure and the sensitivity that one has in grasping what God wants one to do.

10. How do I start discerning seriously?

One does this best by prayer, by asking God in humility and docility what His intentions are for oneself. It is repeating deep in one's heart, "What is Your will, O God, for me? What do you want me to do? I beg Your help in finding out, what is Your intention on my behalf?"

11. What are the preconditions to my discovering my vocation?

Obviously, various vocations demand various qualifications. One needs to have certain assets in order to be called to a particular state in life or arrangement for one's life. The first would be the physical capacity to do whatever kinds of work the vocation might entail. For example, the priesthood and religious life generally require a sound physical capacity, free from serious physical handicaps. Were such handicaps to be present, one would usually suppose that, because of those disabilities, God does not intend that person suffering from those handicaps to be a priest or religious, but has another intention. Also, it is necessary to have the basic moral qualities of living one's life in conformity with God's will, His commandments, and the Catholic faith. In a certain sense, a correct and proper moral life is a prerequisite for every vocation. For some vocations, of course, the intensity of that moral living would (in certain respects) be more important than for others. Everyone is required at least to walk in what is called the purgative way, that is, general freedom from mortal sin and frequent reception of the Sacrament of Reconciliation. The illuminative way is when one is also struggling against venial sins and having some success in eliminating them from one's life. At least those who are called to the vocation of priesthood or religious life should be at the entrance of the illuminative way. The unitive way, which is the way of infused contemplation, is a special gift of God for only certain people.

12. How do I know what my vocation is?

A person can never know their vocation with absolute certitude, but one can come to great moral certitude about his or her vocation. In fact, for some people God's action is very direct and the certitude is virtually perfect. For instance, we can think about how Saint Paul was called by God to his vocation by being struck down near the gate of Damascus, and being told directly by the voice of Christ what he was to do and where he was to go.

Very few vocations are given by God in such a direct and miraculous way. But if we use the normal tools of discernment and submit ourselves to God's will, and place ourselves in trusting and total dependence on God, the result will usually be a great deal of certitude about what God is intending for our lives.

13. Is it possible to make a decision for my entire life?

It most certainly is possible to do that. This truth runs contrary to current cultural norms. Culturally there seems always to be a little hesitation about making a lifelong commitment. Unfortunately, this has adversely affected many vocations, including ones to married life. People suppose they will need to always leave open some door so they can escape into another direction for their lives if they encounter in one particular vocation a measure of sacrifice and discomfort.

14. If God wants me to find my vocation, why doesn't He talk to me more directly?

God does what He wants. It is His will which must prevail and ultimately does prevail in all human activities and, indeed, in all undertakings throughout the universe. Therefore, God approaches me the way He chooses and not the way I might choose. My preferences are irrelevant when I set them against God's will. Since God created us, he knows what the best way to speak to us is.

15. What signs do I need to follow to discover my vocation?

Looking at my physical, moral, intellectual, and psychological characteristics will be the first step to seeing where God wants me to go. How the whole situation of my life exists at the present time can be the basis for looking at vocational signs. Furthermore, there might be a certain inclination or ability that is found in me by someone else—a person who senses that this might be God pointing me in a particular direction He has in mind for me.

16. What signs help me discover my specific vocation in God's plan?

It is those kinds of inclinations and native abilities that will enable me to see sometimes where God intends my life to go. For example, the basic states in life—priesthood, consecrated religious life, a dedicated single (celibate) life in the world, or a married life with possible parenthood—are the fundamentals that a person must view to know where God would want that person to be. Within each of those states of life, a vast variety of other vocations can be exercised. For instance, if somebody has great artistic or musical talent and a great capacity or desire to develop it, such assets could be employed in any of those states in life. One thinks of the desire to share the Faith with others so as to be a missionary in one of those states of life. People with scientific abilities, inclinations, and desires could find a place in any of those states in life to use those specific gifts in line with a vocation.

17. What role does prayer play in my discovering of my vocation?

It is, of course, the primary role. We must always conform our will to God's, just as our Savior said in the Garden of Gethsemane: "Not my will but Thy will be done." Our vocations must always be looked at in the same way. It is good to remember that, to paraphrase C. S. Lewis, heaven is populated by people who have said to

God throughout their lives, "Thy will be done," and hell is populated by people who have said throughout their lives, "My will be done" (see *The Great Divorce*, chapter 9).

18. Besides prayer, is there anything else I should do to discover my vocation?

Yes, there are things that can be done. We should ask other people, especially spiritual advisors, our parents, those who are close to us and know us best, to tell us what they think God might want us to do.

It is always good to talk over a vocation situation with people who are living in the particular state in life to which we believe God might be calling us. One should also talk with people who are involved in a particular work or activity within that state of life in which one could visualize oneself. For example, if someone has an inclination to go to medical school to be a doctor, it would be a good idea for them to talk with doctor friends about what is involved in their profession. And for someone aspiring to be a stay-at-home mom, it would be a good idea to talk with friends who are living that life, about what the vocation of wife and mother involves.

19. What proactive things can one do to get closer to discovering one's vocation?

Certainly, reading about the particular state in life to
[whi]ch one recognizes the possibility of a call, and also
[read]ing about the aspects of various states of life which
[poin]t out the direction one might want to go. For example,
[if a] man thinks that God is calling him to the priesthood,
[he co]uld discern if within the priesthood he is inclined
[towa]rd a general, more undifferentiated practice like that
[of a] diocesan priest, or if he is inclined toward teaching or
[miss]ionary work, some specific area in which a particular
[religi]ous order is functioning. Once he has done that, he
[can l]earn more about that particular kind of vocation and
[what] that state in life is like.

How important are role models in the discernment of my vocation?

Role models can be a sort of actual grace coming
[from] the Lord. They can be figures placed by Him in our
[lives] or at least in our knowledge, in such a way that we
[imag]inatively see ourselves in the lives and activities of
[the] persons we so greatly admire.

Certainly, the saints are great role models for us, and
[the] lives of the saints have been influential in many a
[disc]ernment process. Saint Ignatius of Loyola discovered
[his v]ocation by reading lives of the saints. In the lives he

read about, he saw things God might want him to do. There are many ways in which individuals, young ones especially, look idealistically at accomplishers of great things as role models that they can imitate. This also holds true with secular vocations—how many sports models and figures have given boys or girls inspiration toward great accomplishments in athletics? People in the areas of music and entertainment, dancing and the like have inspired many young people to look at those kinds of achievements as possibilities for their own lives. And we can all be inspired by the lives of the great and important people we know and learn about. So the presence or absence of correct role models depends on choices made both by young people and by those who influence young people. Parents and teachers should try to present themselves as role models truly worthy of emulation, good examples of a life well lived.

21. Who should I look to as a role model?

I think all of us can look to the saints and to the Queen of all the saints, the Blessed Virgin Mary, and how in her ordinary life, she became the greatest of all the saints, greater even than all the angels. One can look to great people. Pope John Paul II in his life influenced thousands and millions of young people to draw closer to Christ and pursue whatever vocation God blessed them with, so that they would be faithful and fulfilled Christians—noble and valiant Catholics. How many people have been influenced by the witness of such people as Saint Maximilian Kolbe and Blessed Teresa of Calcutta, or of other wonderful persons whose lives are worthy of imitation and admiration!

22. What happens if I do not discover my vocation, but still live a decent life?

Well, one would hope that every life is a decent life; but that only happens if it is lived in a worthwhile manner. It is generally conceded that the vocation to a state in life or to a particular function within that state is more of an invitation from God than an actual command. Therefore, if a person is careless or haphazard in discerning their vocation, it will not result in a direct punishment from God. Nevertheless, that person will have to live with the consequence of being less happy in this world, and of course in the world to come, than they would have been if they had been more careful in their discernment.

23. What happens if I discover my vocation and do not follow it?

If you do not find your vocation and follow it, then precisely what I just explained will happen. I think it is more a question of less happiness in this present life than a question of eternal unhappiness. Now, we are all called to live in God's life in the state of grace. In Baptism we were called to the Catholic faith, and if we were to defect from that call, we would be eternally punished for that. However, within that general vocation to holiness and to following Christ, we would not be punished, except with less joy, contentment, and fulfillment than we otherwise would have gotten.

24. How can the Bible help me to discover and accept my vocation?

The inspired word of God in Sacred Scripture is an enormous treasure. As Saint Jerome tells us, ignorance of Scripture is ignorance of Christ (*Commentary on Isaiah*, prologue); and it is only in Christ that we can find and discern what God's will is for us. Our reading Sacred Scripture and discerning can be a means by which God indicates the direction He wants our lives to go. Great reverence for Sacred Scripture as it is proclaimed in the liturgical assembly, that is, in the celebration of Holy Mass, is an important way that we can learn God's intentions for us. Many great saints, such as Saint Anthony the Abbot (a/k/a Saint Anthony of the Desert), found God's vocation for them by walking into a church at the precise

the television set or computer and learn to do without that means of communication, that news and entertainment media that is so dominant in so much of the world. It means sometimes accepting cheerfully a certain measure of discomfort for a greater good. If this is done even in small things, the big decisions will come easier. Everything comes easier with a will that is trained to conform to God's will in all times, places, and circumstances.

33. How can I deal with the pressures of the world to live a way of life that is opposed to God's plans?

There is no doubt that not just individuals but the entire world is tainted by original sin, and that the tide of the world pulls us in a direction contrary to what God wants. In the Western culture especially, the three p's of pleasure, possessions, and power are what pull many human beings toward ways of life which are distant from God's intentions in regard to us. It is always good to try to keep a right sense of priorities: of the spiritual over the material, of the supernatural over the natural. If we live, as much as we can, oriented toward heaven, and have that kind of courage and perseverance in prayer that all Christians should have, it will be easier, although not entirely easy, to oppose worldly pressures not to live in the way that we should.

34. What if my vocation requires that I renounce a successful life?

This depends on what one means by "a successful life." If someone means a life of pleasure, comfort, and vast material possessions, this is not the life that Jesus tells us is successful. A life that is in the long run successful is a life that is in conformity with the great beatitudes. To be poor in spirit, meek, clean of heart; to hunger and thirst for justice and righteousness—these are the secrets of a truly successful life. What the world regards as a successful life might appear externally and temporarily to have that aspect of success, but in the end it is a life of failure.

35. What should I do if my family opposes my vocation?

Parents have a very serious responsibility to be concerned about the welfare of their children, and that includes the duty to advise their children about vocational aspects of life. However, parents have no right to impose their views on a child with regard to vocational issues, and this applies to any child, of no matter what age. While parents can and should give advice, it would be sinful for parents to try to impose on a child a vocation of any kind. But with advice, and with prayerful and deeply loving concern for a child, parents can be of assistance in vocational discernment. For their part, children at every age must be brave and willing even to go against the wishes of their family members, parents included, if they are convinced about God's will for them, painful though that may be.

36. What are the key elements of a vocation to marriage?

God calls most of His children to a married life, and blesses them with the joys and satisfactions of the marital union. He also gives to most of these people the great and important role of parenthood.

The normal drive that God has put in human beings to reproduce the human race is what inclines a person to be attracted to members of the opposite sex and to discern if God wants one to be a married person and, hopefully, a parent. After the instinct to self-preservation, the instinct to species preservation is the most powerful instinct that God has put inside of human beings. That instinct is good and holy when it is directed in accordance with God's views of sexual matters. This means there should be great seriousness about those called to marriage, about deciding who one's spouse will be, and about that kind of irrevocable lifelong commitment that is involved in marriage.

Potential spouses should understand that it takes three to get married: a man, a woman, and God. For Catholic Christians, marriage is a sacrament and sign of the union of Christ with His Church, a union that involves not simply irrevocability but also unselfish love, a total mutual self-giving in the context of our divine call to holiness. It is a union in which each of the two partners accepts the responsibility of helping the other and all their children to get to heaven, in and through the one true church, the Catholic Church. Couples should give long and ponderous thought to their solemn vows that involve not simply *better* but also *worse*, not simply *health* but also *sickness* . . .

The *Catechism of the Catholic Church* explains very clearly how a Catholic marriage, a Christian marriage, is a symbol and sign of the great union between Christ and His Church, as Saint Paul also explains in the fifth chapter of his epistle to the Ephesians. In the *Catechism* we read this: "The entire Christian life bears the mark of the spousal love of Christ and the Church. Already Baptism, the entry into the People of God, is a nuptial mystery; it is, so to speak, the nuptial bath which precedes the wedding feast, the Eucharist. Christian marriage in its turn becomes an efficacious sign, the sacrament of the covenant of Christ and the Church. Since it signifies and communicates grace, marriage between baptized persons is a true sacrament of the New Covenant" (*CCC*, no. 1617).

The key element in the Sacrament of Matrimony is that the husband and wife, the spouses, are not simply the recipients of a sacrament, but are actually the ministers who confer the sacrament on each other, by the giving and receiving of marriage consent and vows. It is important to keep in mind that the first and best wedding present which the spouses give to each other is the grace of the sacrament. When, as it should be, the Sacrament of Matrimony is celebrated in the context of the Holy Eucharist, the greatest and most important of all the sacraments (see the *Catechism*, nos. 1324 and 1325), their first meal together as husband and wife is the Body and Blood of Christ in the Eucharist.

Marriage must not be done under constraint. It must be a consent given and received freely, by persons not impeded by any natural or ecclesiastical law from the giving and taking of matrimonial consent. Anyone who feels called to the vocation of marriage should be pondering the teaching of the Catholic Church on the Sacrament of Matrimony. A good way to go about this is to read slowly and carefully—with one's intended, if possible—the *Catechism's* eloquent and beautiful section on Christian marriage and conjugal love.

37. What are the key elements of a vocation to the priesthood?

The Council of Trent set forth very clearly (in Session 23, canon 6) the fact that an internal vocation or call from Christ to the priesthood can only be made certain when it is externalized and vocalized by the authorities of the Catholic Church. *De facto*, a vocation to the priesthood starts becoming certain and completely real when the bishop, at the actual ceremony of ordination, calls out the name of the candidate for the priesthood and the candidate answers that he is present. His declaration is then followed by the bishop's declaring, after receiving assurances that the future priest has been properly trained, that he will ordain this man to the priesthood of Jesus Christ. Once he is a priest, the man will share in the one priesthood of our divine Lord, that unique mediatorship between God and man, in which an ordained ministerial priest is called to share in a most special and particular way.

In the above-cited talk on vocations, our Holy Father, Pope Benedict XVI, said, "In the context of this universal call to holiness, Christ, the High Priest, in His solicitude for the Church, calls individuals in every generation to care for His people. In particular, He calls men to the priestly ministry, to exercise a fatherly function whose source is

God's fatherhood itself. The mission of the priest in the Church is irreplaceable (see Eph 3:14)." Since it is that vital, those who might understand themselves as called to the priesthood, or who are attempting to discern a vocation to the priesthood, should pray ardently and fervently that they might know if it is God's will. Only then will they have the courage, grace, strength, and fortitude to follow that will.

A vocation to the priesthood requires a decent moral life—one which need not be in the highest realms of sanctity immediately, but which is already seriously aimed at that goal. A physical life free of fundamental disabilities is also required. In addition, certain levels of scholastic achievement and intellectual ability are necessary so that the studies mandatory for every priest can be mastered. And then a certain inclination toward the priesthood, even though other inclinations might be present, would be extremely valuable.

Pope Benedict XVI, quoting Pope John Paul's apostolic exhortation *Pastores Dabo Vobis*, says, "The relation of the priest to Jesus Christ, and in him to his Church, is found in the very being of the priest by virtue of his sacramental consecration/anointing and in his activity, that is, in his mission or ministry. In particular, 'the priest minister is the servant of Christ present in the Church as *mystery, communion and mission*. In virtue of his participation in the "anointing" and "mission" of Christ, the priest can continue Christ's prayer, word, sacrifice and salvific action in the Church. In this way, the priest is a *servant of the Church as mystery* because he actuates the Church's sacramental signs of the presence of the Risen Christ' (no. 16)." A man who thinks he might be called by Jesus Christ to the priesthood should ponder very carefully what the Sacrament of Holy Orders is all about, and what the life of a priest involves. Once again, a basic reference would be the *Catechism*; wonderful words about the priesthood are found there (see especially nos. 1544–1553).

38. What are the key elements of a vocation to the consecrated life?

Pope Benedict XVI has expressed this, too, in his words regarding vocations. He says, "Another special vocation which occupies a place of honor in the Church is the call to the consecrated life. Following the example of Mary of Bethany, who 'sat at the Lord's feet and listened to his teaching' (Lk 10:39), many men and women consecrate themselves to a total and exclusive following of Christ. Although they undertake various services in the field of human formation and care of the poor, in teaching or in assisting the sick, they do not consider these activities as the principal purpose of their life, since, as the Code of Canon Law well underlines, 'the first and foremost duty of all religious is to be the contemplation of divine things and assiduous union with God in prayer' (can. 663 §1)."

The Holy Father once again quotes his predecessor, Pope John Paul II—this time his apostolic exhortation *Vita Consecrata*: "'In the Church's tradition religious profession is considered to be a special and fruitful deepening of the consecration received in Baptism, inasmuch as it is the means by which the close union with Christ already begun in Baptism develops in the gift of a fuller, more explicit and authentic configuration to him through the profession of the evangelical counsels' (no. 30)." *Perfectae Caritatis* (the decree of the Second Vatican Council about religious life) and the chapter in *Lumen Gentium* on religious life (chapter 6) are excellent places to study what a vocation to a consecrated life involves and is about. As with a vocation to the priesthood, some maturity and normal physical, mental, and spiritual health are usually required.

39. Is there a vocation to "singlehood" or being single?

The answer to this question is, of course, yes, there is such a vocation, and that vocation, to be authentic, must be chosen freely, without constraint. It cannot be simply that a person is in a perpetual state of indecision about the direction of God's plan for him or her. There are people who remain in this "neutral zone" for a lifetime—persons who for one reason or another find themselves not selected by (or having selected) someone to be a lifelong marriage partner and who more or less by accident remain in the single state. But to be a vocation, the single state must be freely chosen and freely accepted as a call from God to a particular way of life.

Often people who live a single life in the world dedicate themselves in a special way to some particular kind of work, focusing on it with exceptional attention. These people integrate their labors into their prayer life and spiritual attitudes. Single people who have chosen to remain unmarried for the sake of the kingdom of God (see Mt 19:12) are available for many apostolates. These single people can be lay missionaries, dedicated to helping the sick—even sick parents or other relatives—or, with a greater intensity than would otherwise be possible, to such areas as teaching.

Our Holy Father, Pope Benedict XVI, says, "In the mystery of the Church, the mystical Body of Christ, the divine power of love changes the heart of man, making him able to communicate the love of God to his brothers and sisters. Throughout the centuries many men and women, transformed by divine love, have consecrated their lives to the cause of the Kingdom. Already on the shores of the Sea of Galilee, many allowed themselves to be won by Jesus: they were in search of healing in body or spirit, and they were touched by the power of his grace. Others were chosen personally by him and became his apostles. We also find some, like Mary Magdalene and others, who followed him on their own initiative, simply out of love. Like the disciple John, they too found a special place in his heart. These men and women, who knew the mystery of the love of the Father through Jesus, represent the variety of vocations which have always been present in the Church."

40. Once I have discovered and accepted my vocation, what is next?

The next step, depending on which vocation a person discovered and accepted, is to proceed with whatever steps are necessary to find fulfillment and completion in this vocation.

Obviously, if one discerns a vocation to the priesthood, it is necessary to talk to vocation directors either of specific orders or of a diocese. After this step has been taken, then the interested person should seek admission to the appropriate religious training—postulancy and novitiate, or whatever; that which typically marks entrance into a clerical religious order or into the diocesan priesthood.

If one discerns and accepts a vocation to the consecrated life, the particular form of it that one is thinking about should be examined, so that one can go forward with the further discernment and formation processes that are appropriate for that particular type of consecrated life. Some types of consecrated life can also be found in secular institutes and other constructs, even though the majority of them are found in religious orders or communities.

As one searches for a place to live out their consecrated life, the next step is to try and see if a particular religious order or community's charism, inspiration, and focus mesh with their personality and characteristics.

In a religious order there are even further steps on the path to consecration. The progression of commitment begins with postulancy, followed by the novitiate, temporary vows, and then, lastly, the taking of final vows or consecration. These last vows are supposed to be final and irrevocable decisions made in regard to one's vocation.

If the person has discerned a vocation to a single life in the world, it is recommended that that person would have regular and consistent spiritual direction from skilled and learned priests who will be able to assist in the discernment process. These directors can establish various kinds of daily, weekly, monthly, and annual activities that would support, sustain, and nurture that vocation.

41. How do I strengthen a vocation to married life?

One way a person can strengthen a vocation to married life is to have a discussion about the goals and purposes of marriage with the person they intend to have as their lifelong spouse. Good and proper marriage preparation is extraordinarily important, especially in an age where such marriage values as fidelity and exclusiveness are often missed in the surrounding ambience in which young people find themselves. Prayer is very important, prayer together, so that each day after their wedding day the partners can kneel down together at night and pray "Forgive us as we forgive." This practice of prayer will keep the tensions and inevitable kinds of frictions that arise in family life from corroding the wonderful marital covenant. The widespread availability of such wonderful programs as Engaged Encounter, Pre-Cana, and Marriage Encounter is an indication of the kind of support and training young couples can receive in the Catholic Church these days.

42. How do I strengthen a vocation to the priesthood?

A person called to the priesthood needs spiritual direction, and should receive this from skilled priests. Normally, the training period in seminary life, or a scholasticate that follows the completion of formation in a religious institute, provides many opportunities for the kind of strengthening that is absolutely necessary for following Christ's call to be a priest. A man called to the priesthood must grow in the development of his spiritual life and outlook. He must also deepen his religious practices and the quality of his interior and contemplative association with Christ, in Whose priesthood he hopes to be involved.

43. How do I strengthen a vocation to the consecrated life?

In a similar way to that of those trying to nurture a vocation to the priesthood, those who are called to live a consecrated life normally receive support and information on how to prepare for their consecration from those who are responsible for their formation. Those preparing to be consecrated by the three vows of poverty, chastity, and obedience can strengthen their vocation in that respect by finding in Christ the Model of obedience, the Model of chastity, and the Model of apostolic poverty. As they gaze upon this vision of our Savior, they can also find myriads of opportunities to beseech Him for His grace. If they live a life of grace, then these wonderful vows can allow them to live a life of joy, happiness, and fulfillment.

44. How do I cope with difficulties and uncertainties that paralyze my discernment?

I think what is most necessary in coping with such difficulties and uncertainties is a vision of life that goes beyond what is available simply in this world. It is important to see that, as Scripture says, we have here no lasting city (see Heb 13:14). We seek one that is to come.

It is always important to understand that every vocation, that is, every life that is worth living, is a vocation to love in some way or another. Priests, consecrated men and women, and dedicated single people living in the world all love in the sublimated sexual way of celibacy. Those who are married love in another kind of way in the context of the marital union.

Every vocation to love involves a measure of sacrifice. The consequence of a vocation that is followed out of love, that is involved in the supernatural love that God has for the human race, which Christ exhibits on the cross, is ultimately a finding of joy, happiness, fulfillment, and completion, even in this world. And the joy we experience here in this world, this antechamber to heaven, pales in comparison to the life of happiness that we will experience in the world to come. But this gratification and these joys are only possible when one walks through the doorway of some sacrifice and some measure of courageous confrontation of discomfort. It is good to say often when looking at our Lord on the cross, "Love does such things." In His sacrifice we can find a certain consolation, since the sacrifices we might be called upon to make might be slight and trivial compared to His.

45. How do I cope with temptations that directly attack the nature of my vocation?

Temptations of all sorts have to be treated in different ways, depending on the circumstances. Sometimes it is best to flee from them and not attempt to confront them. We always should pray in the face of every temptation, whether it's an enticement toward sin or an attempt to deflect us from what God would like us to do or become. It is always best for us to situate ourselves in the divine economy, that is, within God's special plan for us, and to try to see how that plan involves not just ourselves but the salvation of many others. Sometimes a person can forget that there are many others depending on him or her to follow God's will. It may be in God's providential wisdom that the salvation of others might be dependent in large measure on one or the other of us following our God-given call. By doing so, we can be appropriate and proper channels of His grace and love to others.

46. Which devotions, prayers, or saints can help me to discover or live my vocation?

The wonderful thing about the saints is that there is such a great variety of them and that they followed Christ in a great number of different ways. One can, by reading the lives of the saints, almost invariably come upon one who is the perfect role model for the vocation to which one is called. There are saints who are priests. There are saints who are consecrated religious. There are saints who live a dedicated single life in the world. And there are saints who live a married life. Saints from all of these categories are given to us by God not only to pray for us before His face in heaven, but also to be examples and models of the various and wonderful ways in which we can follow

Christ. They can teach us how to use the personalities and characteristics with which God has endowed us, and help us to understand the experiences and past sectors of our lives that we bring to bear on our future.

47. What passages of Holy Scripture are good to meditate on?

With regard to vocations, it is always good to think about the entirety of the New Testament, but the Acts of the Apostles, the 28 chapters of which are easily read, is a good place to start. Certainly, the various passages in Saint Paul's epistles that speak about destiny and predestination are also very precious for one who is in a discernment process regarding a vocation. Also, the teachings of our Lord, and especially the summonses of the apostles, which can be seen in all four of the Gospels, would be a very wonderful place to start a meditative study of vocation in the Holy Scriptures.

The Old Testament too has many inspiring passages, including the various calls of the prophets, such as Jeremiah and Isaiah, and the calls of the Judges to a particular kind of activity. One thinks of the summons of Gideon, and the response given to God's call by so many heroic people, such as Abraham and the other patriarchs.

48. What acts of mercy or other activities can help me to identify my vocation?

I think that what one brings by way of experience to the discernment process can certainly be helpful in making a passage to a committed state of life. The works of mercy that are obligatory for all Christians—and these are the spiritual as well as the corporal works of mercy—are always a good preliminary to any vocation. If a carrying out of them were to permeate your life, the grace that would come to you as a consequence of this merciful life would add to the sense of fulfillment and enjoyment that you would encounter in your vocation, whatever it might be. Every vocation, if it is a true and authentic call from God, is a call to service, because a vocation in its authenticity is a reflection of Jesus Christ, Who told us Himself (see Mt 20:28) that He came down to earth not to be served but to serve.

49. What is the secret to perseverance in my vocation?

There is really no secret. What perseverance is, is hitching up one's will to God's will and staying hitched up to God's will. As I mentioned earlier (see question 13), the culture in which we currently live does not lend itself to heroic and lifelong commitments, and this might account for some of the shallow and short-term commitments one finds in those who start out on the way that God has designated for them and then turn back. It is always best to bear in mind Jesus' statement that whoever takes hold of the plow and looks back is not worthy of Him and not fit to enter into the kingdom of God (see Lk 9:62). Perseverance means going always and ever forward. When someone whom the Lord had summoned to follow Him came up with the excuse, "I must go and bury the dead," He told him to let the dead bury the dead (see Lk 9:60). He expects those called by Him to look forward to the future, a future of life, rather than make excuses.

In the conclusion of the above-mentioned discourse on vocations, the Holy Father said, "The holiness of the Church depends essentially on union with Christ and on being open to the mystery of grace that operates in the hearts of believers." There could probably be no clearer, more concise, or more eloquent expression of what is involved in the call, the summons of God which goes by the designation *vocation*.

The Shepherd's Voice Series

The Shepherd's Voice Series brings you the current teachings of Bishops and Cardinals on vital topics facing the Catholic Church today.

Catholics in the Public Square
Bishop Thomas J. Olmsted of Phoenix explains the rights and duties we Catholics have as citizens, and what is and is not appropriate for us to do within the secular realm. He also describes how we should seek to influence our nation and its political processes in light of our Catholic faith.

A Will to Live: Clear Answers on End of Life Issues
Archbishop José Gomez of San Antonio, Texas, renowned expert on death-and-dying issues, explains how to approach these issues and prepare for death in a moral way, consistent with our Catholic faith.

Draw Near to Me: Heartfelt Prayers for Everyday Life
Francis Cardinal Arinze explains the power of prayer, describes how to pray, and gives examples of prayers we can use for life's triumphs and challenges. This magnificent, user-friendly work will comfort and inspire anyone seeking an ever closer relationship with the Holy Trinity.

What God Has Joined: A Catholic Teaching on Marriage
In this pastoral book, Bishop Kevin W. Vann explains what every Catholic needs to know about the Church's teachings on marriage and about the often confusing issues surrounding Matrimony at a time when values seem to change by the day. This booklet is essential for engaged couples, married couples, single laypersons, priests, and religious.

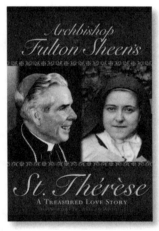

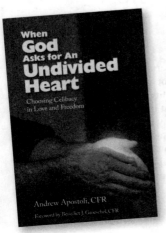